MW01101143

DEC   2012

Canada's Political Parties

THE CONSERVATIVE PARTY

Douglas and Patricia Baldwin

Weigl

Published by Weigl Educational Publishers Limited
6325 10th Street SE
Calgary, Alberta
T2H 2Z9

Website: www.weigl.ca

Library and Archives Canada Cataloguing in Publication

Baldwin, Douglas, 1944-
        Conservative Party / Douglas and Patricia Baldwin.

(Canada's political parties)
Includes index.
ISBN 978-1-77071-695-7 (bound).--ISBN 978-1-77071-700-8 (pbk)

        1. Conservative Party of Canada. I. Baldwin, Patricia, 1946-
II. Title. III. Series: Canada's political parties (Calgary, Alta.)

JL197.C75B35 2011   j324.271'094   C2011-900815-7

Printed in the United States of America in North Mankato, Minnesota
1 2 3 4 5 6 7 8 9 0 15 14 13 12 11

072011
WEP040711

Project Coordinator: Heather Kissock
Design: Terry Paulhus

Photograph Credits
CP Images: pages 13TL, 13TR, 15BL, 17BL, 17BR, 18, 19TL, 19BL, 21TL, 21TR, 21B, 24B, 25M, 27; Dreamstime: page 4; Getty Images: pages 6R, 7TR, 7BR, 7BL, 9TL, 9TR, 9B, 11B, 12, 13BL, 13BR, 15BR, 16, 17TL, 19TR, 19BR, 20, 22BR, 24TR, 25TL, 25TR, 25BL, 25BR, 25TR, 26; Glenbow Museum: pages 11TL, 11TR, 14; Library and Archives Canada: pages 6L, 8, 10, 17TR, 24TL, 24TM, 24M.

Every reasonable effort has been made to trace ownership and to obtain permission to reprint copyright material. The publishers would be pleased to have any errors or omissions brought to their attention so that they may be corrected in subsequent printings.

We acknowledge the financial support of the Government of Canada through the Canada Book Fund for our publishing activities.

CONTENTS

Overview of Canada's Political Parties

Political parties in Canada are made up of people with similar beliefs who have joined together to accomplish specific goals. To achieve these goals, the party attempts to elect enough members to gain control of the government.

Political parties are central to Canada's political system. In their attempts to win elections, parties propose a series of social, economic, and political policies called the party platform. The election campaign then attempts to convince the people to vote for candidates who support these beliefs. This process provides the people with a way of expressing their opinions and of holding the winning party accountable for its actions.

Beginnings

The first Canadian political parties started in central Canada in the 1820s and 1830s. They were created to ensure that the people's wishes were presented to the British governor who ruled the **colonies**. The achievement of **responsible government** in the late 1840s paved the way for the emergence of party politics as they are known today. When Canada became a nation in 1867, there was only the Liberal Party and the Conservative Party. These two parties dominated politics until the 1920s. The rise of the Progressive Party in the 1920s, and the emergence of the Co-operative Commonwealth Federation and the Social Credit parties in the 1930s gave voters more choices through which to express their concerns. However, these "third" parties never seriously challenged the power of the two major parties.

This situation changed, however, in the 1980s. The Reform Party began in 1987 as an alternative to the Progressive Conservative Party. In 2000, it transformed into the Canadian Alliance, which then merged with the Progressive Conservative Party in 2003 to form the Conservative Party. Today, the Conservative Party, Liberal Party, New Democratic Party (NDP), Green Party, and Bloc Québécois compete to dominate Canadian politics.

In Canada, federal, provincial, and municipal governments discuss and make decisions about many activities that affect the daily lives of citizens.

The Parliament Buildings in Ottawa have been the centre of Canadian politics since 1867.

The Conservative Party—
Its Beliefs and Philosophy

The Conservative Party has undergone major changes since its creation in 1854, with most of these changes happening within the last 20 years. The merger of the Progressive Conservative Party and the Canadian Alliance in 2003 created a new party with a new approach to the Conservative mandate. For more than 140 years, the party had desired a strong central government in Ottawa, preferred **tariffs** rather than free trade, created government-funded social programs, and wanted a close attachment to Great Britain.

The new Conservative Party of 2003 favoured lower taxes, **private enterprise**, smaller government, more **decentralization** of federal government powers to the provinces, a stronger military, privatization of public services, and a tougher stand on "law and order" issues.

Founding Principles

At the 2005 Conservative convention, the party set forth its "Founding Principles." Following are a few of the beliefs and goals found within the document.

- "A balance between fiscal accountability, progressive social policy and individual rights and responsibilities;
- A belief in the equality of all Canadians;
- A belief in the freedom of the individual, including freedom of speech, worship and assembly;
- A belief in our **constitutional monarchy**, the institutions of Parliament and the democratic process;
- A belief in the federal system of government as the best expression of the diversity of our country, and in the desirability of strong provincial and territorial governments..."

Registering a Political Party

1. Political parties do not have to be registered with the government. However, registered parties can provide tax receipts for donations, thus saving the donors money. An official party can place its name beneath its candidates' names on the ballot.

2. To be registered, a party must:
- Have statements from at least 250 individuals who are qualified to vote (i.e. 18 years old and a Canadian citizen) indicating that they are party members
- Endorse (sponsor) at least one candidate in a general election or a by-election
- Have at least three officers, in addition to the party leader, who live in Canada and are eligible to vote

- Have an auditor
- Submit a copy of the party's resolution appointing its leader
- Have an agent who is qualified to sign contracts
- Submit a letter stating that party will support one or more of its members as candidates for election

3. The party's name, abbreviation, or logo (if any) must not resemble those of any other party and must not include the word "independent." Once the Chief Electoral Officer has verified the party's application (confirming that 250 electors are members of the party and that the party has met all the other requirements), and is satisfied that the party's name and logo will not be confused with those of another registered or eligible party, he or she will inform the party leader that the party is eligible for registration.

Source: Elections Canada

Conservative Party Leaders

Canada has had a Conservative Party in one form or another since **Confederation**. Through the course of Canadian history, the Conservatives won many federal elections, and, as a result, several Conservative leaders have assumed the position of prime minister.

NAME	TERM	NAME	TERM
John Abbott	1891–1892	Joe Clark	1976–1983
John Thompson	1892–1894	Erik Nielsen	1983
Mackenzie Bowell	1894–1896	Brian Mulroney	1983-1993
Charles Tupper	1896–1901	Kim Campbell	1993
Robert Laird Borden	1901–1920	Jean Charest	1993-1998
Arthur Meighen	1920–1926	Elsie Wayne	1998
Hugh Guthrie	1926–1927	Joe Clark	1998-2003
Richard Bedford Bennett	1927–1938	Peter MacKay	2003
Robert Manion	1938–1940	John Lynch-Staunton	2003-2004
Richard Hanson	1940–1941	Stephen Harper	2004-Present
Arthur Meighen	1941–1942		
John Bracken	1942–1948		
George Drew	1948–1956		
John George Diefenbaker	1956–1967		
Robert Stanfield	1967–1976		

FIRST PRIME MINISTER
JOHN A. MACDONALD
1815–1891

Macdonald was born in Scotland and came to Canada with his parents when he was five years old. He was elected to the Assembly in 1844. Macdonald's intelligence and knowledge of politics soon made him one of the leading politicians in Canada. Following Confederation, he became Canada's first prime minister, serving from 1867 to 1873. He served a second term from 1878 to 1891. With a total of 18 years in office, he is the second-longest serving Canadian prime minister, after William Lyon Mackenzie King of the Liberal Party.

Macdonald was often called Canada's Patriot Statesman due to his commitment to governing the country.

EIGHTH PRIME MINISTER
ROBERT LAIRD BORDEN
1854–1897

Borden came from a farming family in Nova Scotia. He excelled in school and, at the age of 14, became an assistant school master. By 19, Borden was teaching school in New Jersey. He became bored with teaching, however, and returned to Nova Scotia to become a lawyer. Borden was elected to Parliament in 1896 and became prime minister in 1911. Dealing with Canada's role in World War I exhausted Borden. At the war's conclusion, doctors advised him to quit politics immediately. Sir Robert Laird Borden died on June 10, 1937.

After leaving politics, Borden became the chancellor of Queen's University. He held this position from 1924 to 1929.

ELEVENTH PRIME MINISTER

RICHARD BEDFORD BENNETT
1870–1947

Bennett was born in New Brunswick. He was a good student, and by age 18, he was the principal of four schools. By 1890, Bennett had saved enough money to study law at Dalhousie University in Nova Scotia. After graduation, he moved to Calgary, Alberta. In 1911, Bennett was elected to the House of Commons. Disappointed at not being made a Cabinet minister, he refused to run in the 1917 election, but returned to the House of Commons in 1925 and became prime minister five years later. After resigning as party leader in 1938, Bennett moved to England and sat in the House of Lords. He died in England in 1947.

Bennett was known as a charitable man. He donated up to $25,000 each year to charities.

THIRTEENTH PRIME MINISTER

JOHN GEORGE DIEFENBAKER
1895–1979

Diefenbaker's early life was spent moving from one town to another as his father sought teaching jobs. Following high school, Diefenbaker attended the University of Saskatchewan, where he received bachelor and master of arts degrees. After serving in World War I, Diefenbaker returned to university and earned a law degree. Diefenbaker's political success was a tribute to persistence. He lost in two attempts to enter the House of Commons. In 1929, he failed to win the provincial election. He twice failed to become Progressive Conservative Party leader before he won in 1956. His funeral, which he planned himself, was one of the most elaborate in Canadian history.

Diefenbaker continued to represent his Prince Albert riding in the House of Commons until his death in 1979.

EIGHTEENTH PRIME MINISTER

MARTIN "BRIAN" MULRONEY
1939–

Mulroney became involved in politics when he enrolled at St. Francis Xavier University in Nova Scotia. After graduating with a law degree from Laval University, he joined a prominent Montreal law firm. He became leader of the Conservative Party in 1983 and was elected prime minister the following year. He held this position until 1993. After leaving office, Mulroney served as an international business consultant and lawyer and sat on the board of directors of multiple corporations.

When he was only 17 years old, Mulroney worked on Diefenbaker's 1956 campaign to become prime minister. The campaign was a success.

TWENTY-SECOND PRIME MINISTER

STEPHEN JOSEPH HARPER
1959–

Harper became a member of the Young Liberal's Club in high school in Toronto. He earned his Master of Arts in economics at the University of Calgary. Harper became a member of the Progressive Conservative Party, but moved to the Reform Party in 1986. In 1993, he was elected to Parliament. In 2002, he became leader of the Canadian Alliance. When the Alliance merged with the Progressive Conservatives, Harper became party leader. He was elected prime minister in 2006.

Harper moved to Calgary in 1978 to work in the petroleum industry. It was here that he obtained his bachelor's and master's degrees in economics.

Louis Riel was the leader of the Northwest Rebellion of 1885. The two-month battle ultimately led to his death.

The Macdonald Era, 1867–1891

Sir John A. Macdonald and George-Étienne Cartier founded the Conservative Party in 1854. It was called the Liberal-Conservative Party until 1873. When Canada became the first **dominion** in the British Empire on July 1, 1867, John A. Macdonald became Canada's first prime minister.

In the next few years, Macdonald brought Manitoba, British Columbia, and Prince Edward Island into Confederation. The Conservative Party also built a transcontinental railway to link the provinces together and to make the settlement of the Prairies possible.

In the 1878 election, the Conservatives campaigned on what they called the "National Policy"—a tariff on imported goods. Thanks to support for both the railway and the tariff, the Conservative Party won the 1878, 1882, 1887, and 1891 elections.

One of Macdonald's most difficult challenges was the execution of Louis Riel. In 1885, the **Métis** felt that their way of life was being endangered by railways, settlers, and Canadian laws and culture. They asked Riel to negotiate with Ottawa. Riel agreed, but when Macdonald refused to help, Riel armed his men, formed a government, and demanded the surrender of Fort Carlton. After two months of fighting, Riel surrendered.

Riel was charged with **treason**, which carried the death sentence. The jury found Riel guilty but recommended clemency. Macdonald now had to decide whether Riel should be executed. English Canadians demanded that Riel hang. French Canadians urged Macdonald to pardon him. Macdonald and his Cabinet decided that Riel deserved to hang.

This decision had a major influence on Canadian history. In the 1887 election, French-Canadian support for the party declined. In Quebec, the provincial Conservative Party was defeated. This paved the way for the Liberal Party's victory in the federal election of 1896.

> When Canada became the first dominion in the British Empire on July 1, 1867, Sir John A. Macdonald became Canada's first prime minister.

FREE TRADE OR TARIFFS?

In 1891, Macdonald fought his last election. Canada was in the midst of an **economic depression**. The Liberal Party campaigned for **free trade** with the United States. The Conservative Party claimed that free trade would give the United States the opportunity to undersell Canadian goods, which would negatively impact the Canadian economy. The Conservative Party argued that tariffs on imported goods would be better for Canadians. The voters had to decide which party to support.

CONSERVATIVE

Tariffs on imported goods from the United States would increase their price. This would allow Canadian companies to compete with U.S. manufacturers who were underselling them. The Canadian companies would then hire workers and provide employment for Canadians. If Canada allowed cheaper American goods to enter the country, the United States would soon control Canada.

LIBERAL

The Conservative government had imposed tariffs on imported goods since 1879—why would they work now? Without tariffs on imported goods, American products would be cheaper. This would allow Canadians to buy more goods. With free trade, Canada would be able to sell its natural resources, such as timber, fish, and agricultural goods, to the United States.

THE RESULT

The Conservatives won the election because Macdonald convinced the people that the issue was national survival. In a famous speech, Macdonald declared, "A British subject I was born—a British subject I will die. With my utmost effort, with my latest breath, will I oppose the 'veiled treason'[of the Liberal Party]."

Conservative Legacy

Under John A. Macdonald, the Conservative Party expanded Canada from coast to coast.

1. It constructed the Canadian Pacific Railway.
2. It encouraged settlers to head west.
3. It created the North-West Mounted Police to protect settlers and maintain order.
4. The Conservatives held discussions and signed treaties with **First Nations**.

The driving of the last spike on November 7, 1885, completed the construction of the Canadian Pacific Railway. The railway's construction played a key role in British Columbia joining Confederation.

Years of Uncertainty, 1891–1896

When John A. Macdonald died in office in 1891, the Conservative Party fell into disarray. Over the next five years, there were four Conservative prime ministers. The first, John Abbott, held the position for about 17 months before resigning due to health problems.

John Thompson, a respected judge, replaced Abbott. Many people thought that Thompson would become prime minister after Macdonald died. However, Thompson declined the position. The country was predominantly English Protestant at the time, and he was Roman Catholic. There were concerns that people would not vote for him. He finally assumed the prime ministerial position in 1892. His term in office ended abruptly, however, when he died of a heart attack in 1894.

Mackenzie Bowell was the third prime minister to follow Macdonald. He had the misfortune to be the leader during the Manitoba Schools controversy over religious and bilingual instruction. The debate over the issue spanned five years, and ultimately cost Bowell his job. He was replaced as leader by Charles Tupper.

Tupper never got the chance to show what he could do. The Conservatives' five-year term in office was over, and it was time for an election. The country was tired of the Conservative Party, with its frequent leadership changes. The Liberal candidate, Wilfrid Laurier, was popular in Quebec. As a result, the Liberal Party won the 1896 election.

> **Over the next five years, there were four Conservative prime ministers.**

❧ The Manitoba Schools controversy was not only an issue between French and English or the Protestant and Roman Catholic religions. It also highlighted the struggle between provincial and federal jurisdiction.

FUNDING FOR SEPARATE SCHOOLS

When Manitoba became a province in 1870, the federal government created two publicly-funded educational systems—a Protestant system taught in English and a Catholic system taught in French. Twenty years later, the provincial government of Thomas Greenway created a single public school system taught in English and ended funding for Catholic schools. After years of court cases, the court ruled in 1895 that the federal government had the right to restore funding to Manitoba's Catholic schools. The question was, should it force Manitoba to cancel its law?

YES

French Canadians in Manitoba and Quebec saw the 1890 law as an attack on the rights of both Roman Catholics and French Canadians. The laws of Manitoba and the British North America Act stated that the minority had a right to have their education and language rights protected.

NO

When Manitoba became a province in 1870, its population was almost equally divided between Catholics and Protestants. In the 20 years that followed, English Protestant settlers flooded into the province and now greatly outnumbered the French and Catholic inhabitants. It was becoming too expensive to fund two separate educational systems. Education was a provincial matter in which the federal government should not interfere.

THE RESULT

When Bowell decided to force Manitoba to repeal the law, several Cabinet members revolted against his leadership, and the government ground to a halt. They only returned when Bowell promised to resign and let Charles Tupper become prime minister. The issue was not resolved until after the Liberals won the next election. At that time, Wilfrid Laurier, the Liberal prime minister, worked out a compromise with the Manitoba government that allowed bilingual and religious instruction under certain conditions.

Conservative Legacy

Due to the upheaval, the Conservative Party's accomplishments during this time were limited. Under Thompson, however, the government passed a new **Criminal Code**, which included the following features.

1. Juveniles were distinguished from adults and given lesser punishments.
2. Suspects were given the right to testify on their own behalf.

Today, courts across the country, including the Supreme Court of Canada, rely on the Criminal Code to make their judgments.

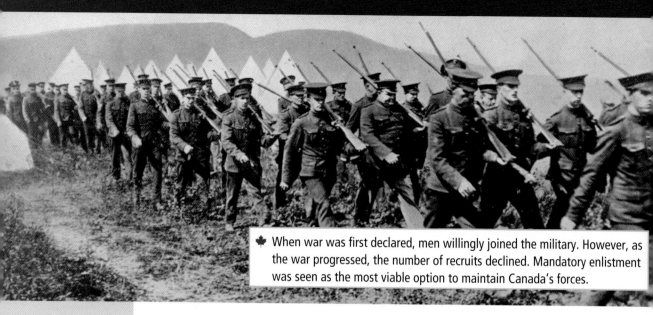

🍁 When war was first declared, men willingly joined the military. However, as the war progressed, the number of recruits declined. Mandatory enlistment was seen as the most viable option to maintain Canada's forces.

Return to Power, 1911–1921

When Tupper resigned as leader of the Conservatives in 1901, Robert Borden was reluctant to become the leader of the Conservative Party. He felt he lacked the experience and qualifications the position needed. He accepted the position only out of a sense of duty to the country.

Borden spent the next 10 years rebuilding the party. Although he did not have Laurier's speaking charisma, he was very efficient and worked hard. When Borden lost the next two elections to the Liberals, his colleagues began to doubt his leadership abilities. However, in 1911, Borden became prime minister.

The 1911 election in English Canada was dominated by the issue of **reciprocity**. Since the 1800s, the idea of free trade with the U.S. had appealed to some Canadians and angered others. Those who supported free trade argued that it would create jobs in Canada and be good for the economy. Other people opposed free trade on the grounds that it would be a first step toward Canada becoming part of the U.S. When Laurier proposed a reciprocity treaty with the United States in 1911,

the Conservative Party accused Laurier of giving away Canada's economic and political independence.

Borden's leadership ability was tested during World War I. Canadian factories were not equipped to produce guns, bullets, tanks, or other military equipment. The entire country and its economy had to be readied for war. As casualties mounted and enlistments declined, Borden felt increasing pressure to adopt **conscription**. He called an election to resolve the issue. The Liberals captured 62 of the 65 seats in Quebec, but only 20 **constituencies** outside Quebec. Borden won, but Canada was divided along French-English lines. For the next 40 years, most French Canadians refused to vote Conservative.

Borden resigned in 1920, two years after the war ended. The party selected Arthur Meighen to replace him.

> **Borden's leadership ability was tested during World War I.**

CONSCRIPTION CRISIS

In the face of mounting casualties and declining enlistments, Borden proposed that eligible Canadians be forced to enlist in the armed forces. To push the proposal through Parliament, he asked Wilfrid Laurier to form a **coalition government** with the Conservatives. When Laurier rejected the offer, Borden convinced the English-speaking Liberal members of Parliament (MPs) to join him in a coalition government and called an election for December 17, 1917. The issue was simple—conscription or not?

YES

NO

Canadian soldiers were dying overseas fighting for Great Britain. Without reinforcements, which were declining quickly, many more would die, and Germany would win the war. Democracy would be defeated by German militarism. "Our first duty," Borden said, "is to win at any cost."

Unlike English Canadians, French Canadians had no ties with Britain. They also felt little attachment to France. The war did not concern Canadians. There was more need for men at home to better the economy. Canadians should not be forced to enlist.

THE RESULT

Borden took the vote away from those people he thought did not want conscription (recent immigrants from Germany) and gave the vote to people who favoured it (wives, mothers, sisters of soldiers, and women in the armed forces). Borden won the election. Approximately 125,000 men were conscripted, but only 25,000 of these saw action.

Borden's Conservatives had several successes during their time in office.

1. As a result of Canada's war effort, the country gained recognition from Great Britain and the world, a role at the **Versailles peace talks**, and a seat at the **League of Nations**.
2. With the exception of Aboriginal and Asian women, the Conservatives gave women over 21 years of age the right to vote in federal elections.
3. They established Income Tax and daylight savings time.
4. They created the national Department of Health.

The League of Nations was created following World War I. One of its main goals was to provide a setting for governments to air and solve problems before they escalated into violence.

Initially, income tax was intended as a temporary measure to get the country through the lean war years.

Years of Despair, 1921–1957

In July 1920, Arthur Meighen became prime minister. He inherited a country still reeling from the aftereffects of the war. Strikes, unemployment, inflation, and regional divisions ruled the land. The Liberal Party thus easily won the 1921 election. During the next four years, Meighen worked hard to rebuild the party, and in the election of 1925, the party won more seats than the Liberals. However, Liberal leader William Lyon Mackenzie King retained power by forming an alliance with the Progressive Party.

In 1926, the governor general made Arthur Meighen prime minister when a scandal rocked the Liberal government. The Liberal Party had asked the governor general, Lord Byng, to dissolve Parliament and call an election, but Byng asked the Conservative Party to form the government instead. Four days later, the Conservatives lost a **vote of confidence** in the House of Commons. Meighen asked Byng to dissolve Parliament and call an election. In the resulting election campaign, King accused Byng of interfering in Canadian politics. The voters agreed and gave the Liberals a majority victory. Meighen resigned as Conservative leader and was replaced by R. B. Bennett in 1927.

> **Bennett poured all his energies into fighting the Depression.**

Bennett's chance to form the government came in 1930. He became prime minister as the world plummeted into the **Great Depression**. Bennett poured all his energies into fighting the Depression. He immediately provided $20 million for the unemployed. To protect Canadian jobs, he put high tariffs on imported goods. The lines outside the soup kitchens only grew longer. Bennett could not end the Depression. No one could. In the 1935 election, the Conservatives were voted out of office.

For the next two decades, the Conservative Party struggled to find a suitable leader who could overcome French Canadians' reluctance to vote Conservative and unite the party. When Robert J. Manion led the party to only 40 seats in the 1940 election, he was replaced by Arthur Meighen. Two years later, Manitoba Premier John Bracken became party leader. Bracken accepted the leadership on the condition that the Conservative Party add the word "Progressive" to its name. Three years after the Progressive Conservatives lost the 1945 election, Ontario Premier George Drew replaced Bracken. He did no better, losing elections in 1949 and 1953. Drew's resignation in 1956 set the stage for John Diefenbaker's success the following year.

🍁 During the Bennett years, few people could afford fuel for their cars. The cars were pulled by oxen instead. These vehicles became known as Bennett buggies.

DEPRESSION OR NOT?

The tremendous economic growth during the 1920s convinced almost everyone that good times were here to stay. Canada's stock market boomed, and from 1921 to 1929, stock prices tripled. It all came to an end on "**Black Tuesday**," October 29, 1929. Almost overnight, individuals and companies were ruined. In the 1930 election, Canadians had to decide whether to vote for the existing Liberal government of Mackenzie King, or the Conservative Party of R.B. Bennett.

VOTE KING

King did not believe the economic situation was serious. Canada's economy had been booming for the past five years. The situation would turn itself around. Providing relief for the unemployed was not the responsibility of the federal government. When the provincial premiers asked for money to fight unemployment, King stated that he would not give "a five-cent piece" to any Conservative provincial government.

VOTE BENNETT

Bennett campaigned on a platform of aggressive measures to combat unemployment and the Depression. He promised to greatly increase Canada's tariffs on imports to force other countries to lower their tariffs on Canada's exports. "I propose that any government of which I am the head will at the first session of parliament initiate whatever action is necessary to that end, or perish in the attempt."

THE RESULT

Bennett spent a great deal of his own fortune on the election. This was the first federal election in which the radio played an important role, and Bennett's radio voice was much better than King's. In August 1930, Canadians elected Richard Bedford Bennett prime minister. They hoped that he would be able to improve Canada's economic situation. Unfortunately, it was the worst depression in history.

Conservative Legacy

Under Bennett, the Conservative Party developed several institutions and social programs.

1. It created the Canadian Radio Broadcasting Commission, a forerunner to the Canadian Broadcasting Corporation.
2. It was also responsible for establishing the Bank of Canada, the Canadian Wheat Board, and the Unemployment Relief Act, which established government responsibility for helping those in need.

The Bank of Canada is Canada's central bank. It is responsible for keeping the country's rate of inflation under control.

The Canadian Wheat Board allows farmers to control the marketing of its barley and wheat. All revenue from the sale of these crops, minus marketing costs, is returned to the farmers.

The Diefenbaker Era, 1957–1968

Diefenbaker injected new energy and ideas into the Progressive Conservative Party. Canada had never seen a campaigner like him. On the strength of his personality, the Progressive Conservative Party was able to win 112 seats in the 1957 election and form a **minority government**.

When the new Liberal leader, Lester Pearson, stated that the Conservative Party should hand power back to the Liberals, Diefenbaker called a snap election in 1958. The Progressive Conservatives won by a record number of seats.

Diefenbaker wanted to create a nation in which all citizens were treated equally.

Diefenbaker wanted to create a nation in which all citizens were treated equally. He gave Aboriginal Peoples the right to vote in federal elections without having to give up their **treaty and status rights**. He improved social programs to provide more aid for the needy. He abolished **racial quotas** for immigrants, and for the first time, Canada accepted larger numbers of Asian and Black immigrants.

Economic problems and indecision plagued the Conservative government. Unemployment rose, while the value of the Canadian dollar declined to 92.5 cents (U.S.). In the 1962 election, the Progressive Conservatives were reduced to a minority government.

Months after the election, Diefenbaker clashed with U.S. president John F. Kennedy. When Russian nuclear missiles were discovered in Cuba, President Kennedy blockaded the island to stop Soviet ships and airplanes from delivering offensive weapons. Canada received only a few hours' warning of the blockade, and Diefenbaker was annoyed at not being consulted. The Canadian government delayed placing its air force on the highest alert, and Diefenbaker refused to send the naval fleet to sea. Americans were angry, and many Canadians were appalled that the government had not co-operated in such a dangerous situation.

Diefenbaker's government began to fall apart. Early in 1963, several cabinet members demanded that Diefenbaker resign. When three members resigned, the opposition toppled the government with a vote of non-confidence in the House of Commons. In the ensuing election, the Liberals won, and Lester Pearson became prime minister of another minority government. Two years later, another election resulted in a Liberal minority again.

The Progressive Conservative Party was floundering. In 1967, party president Dalton Camp called a leadership convention. At the convention, Robert Stanfield was chosen as party leader.

NUCLEAR WEAPONS FOR CANADA

In 1957, Diefenbaker committed Canada to participation in the North American Air Defence Agreement (NORAD). The following year, as part of Canada's NORAD commitment, he agreed to accept missiles from the U.S. and to arm the missiles with nuclear warheads. However, when Canadians began to demonstrate against the warheads, Diefenbaker stalled on the agreement. The issue created an uproar in the House of Commons, and the opposition parties forced an election in 1963.

YES TO WARHEADS

The Liberals felt that Canada had to fulfill its commitment to NORAD. Lester Pearson stated that, because Diefenbaker had promised the United States government that Canada would accept and arm the missiles with nuclear warheads, Canada was morally committed to do so. The situation was straining Canada-U.S. relations. Accepting the warheads would ease the tension.

NO TO WARHEADS

Diefenbaker was concerned that Canadians were not receptive to having nuclear warheads on their soil. He also felt that the U.S. was not showing the proper respect to Canada on this issue and others. He wanted to assert Canada's right to make its own decisions. As a result, he refused to arm the missiles with nuclear warheads and chose conventional warheads instead.

THE RESULT

The Liberals won a minority government, and Pearson agreed to accept nuclear warheads for the missiles. In 1969, new Prime Minister Pierre Trudeau began to phase out the nuclear weapons with an end date of 1971.

Under Diefenbaker, the Progressive Conservatives had many achievements.

1. Diefenbaker developed a **Bill of Rights** for all Canadians.
2. The party reduced discrimination in Canada's immigration policies.
3. The Progressive Conservatives expanded voting rights for Aboriginal Peoples.
4. The Conservatives developed new export markets for prairie wheat in China.

Prior to the Diefenbaker years, Canada restricted people of certain racial backgrounds from immigrating to Canada. Today, people of all races have the opportunity to become Canadian citizens.

Diefenbaker's Bill of Rights became law in 1960. It set forth rights that were to be shared by all Canadians.

A Long Road to Victory, 1968–1993

Stanfield's popularity soon had the Conservative Party leading the polls. Many people expected that he would defeat Pearson's Liberals in the next election. However, when Pierre Trudeau replaced Pearson as party leader, the Conservative Party was overwhelmed in the 1968 election. After failing to win the next two elections as well, Stanfield resigned as leader in 1976.

The new leader, Joe Clark, also found it difficult to compete with Trudeau's charismatic image. However, in 1979, the Conservative Party formed a minority government. At the age of 39, Clark became Canada's youngest prime minister. When he announced plans to raise gasoline taxes, the opposition parties passed a vote of non-confidence, and the Conservative government lost the subsequent election. Clark had been prime minister for only nine months.

To silence his critics, Clark called for a leadership convention in 1983. To his surprise, the party elected Brian Mulroney. When an election was held the next year, Mulroney led the Conservatives to the largest **majority government** in Canadian history. It was the party's first majority government in 26 years. Four years later, the Conservatives won another majority.

Mulroney is best remembered for the Meech Lake Accord, which was his attempt to solve Quebec's unhappiness with Confederation. In April 1987, Mulroney and the provincial leaders met at Meech Lake, in Quebec, to discuss changes to the **Constitution**. The agreement gave the provinces more powers and recognized Quebec as a "distinct society." However, when Manitoba and Newfoundland failed to **ratify** the agreement, the Meech Lake Accord died.

In February 1993, with his popularity at its lowest, Mulroney announced he was retiring from politics. He was replaced by Kim Campbell. Canada's economy was in a slump, and several Conservative MPs had been caught in scandals. Many Canadians were angry with the new Goods and Services Tax (GST) and frustrated with Mulroney's inability to reduce the country's debt and solve Québec's constitutional concerns.

> Mulroney is best remembered for the Meech Lake Accord.

🍁 Prior to the 1983 leadership convention, Joe Clark and Brian Mulroney had campaigned for the leadership of the Progressive Conservative Party in 1976. Mulroney, therefore, was considered Clark's main competition in 1983.

FREE TRADE

Prime Minister Mulroney announced in October 1987 that he had negotiated a deal with the United States to remove tariffs on a long list of goods and services, including meat products, live animals, wine, clothing, and textiles. When the Liberal-dominated Senate refused to ratify the treaty, Mulroney called an election for 1988. The issue of free trade dominated the 1988 federal election.

YES TO FREE TRADE

Mulroney claimed that "our political **sovereignty**, our system of social programs, our commitment to fight regional disparities, our unique cultural identity, our special linguistic character" were not for sale. Free trade, he argued, would provide Canadians with access to the much larger American market. The Canadian Federation of Independent Business and the Consumers' Association of Canada believed that free trade would bring more jobs and increased prosperity.

NO TO FREE TRADE

The opponents of free trade claimed that it would lead to the end of Canadian independence. Such prominent writers and artists as Margaret Atwood and David Suzuki claimed that it would threaten Canadian cultural industries and social programs. Labour unions also opposed free trade, saying that it would lead to unemployment and lower wages.

THE RESULT

With strong support in Alberta and Quebec, the Conservatives were re-elected and the Canada-U.S. Free Trade Agreement was passed.

Mulroney's government had many achievements during its nine years in power.

1. The Conservatives established two free trade agreements.
2. They passed the Goods and Services Tax (GST).
3. The Conservatives established a Green Plan for a Healthy Environment to clean up Canada's air, water, Arctic, parks, and wildlife.
4. The Conservatives put together the plans that created the territory of Nunavut.

Mulroney was responsible for the Canada-United States Free Trade Agreement in 1988 and negotiated much of the North American Free Trade Agreement, which brought Mexico into the arrangement.

Finance Minister Michael Wilson announced the creation of the GST in the Conservative government's 1991 federal budget.

A New Beginning, 1993–2011

When the Progressive Conservative Party elected Kim Campbell to succeed Mulroney, she became the first Canadian female prime minister. In the next election, the Conservative Party suffered the worst defeat in Canadian history. It fell from 154 to 2 seats and lost its official party status. Campbell resigned as party leader and was replaced by Jean Charest.

Charest inherited a divided party. Many French-Canadians now favoured the Bloc Québécois, and Western conservatives were attracted to the Reform Party. Charest began to rebuild the Progressive Conservative Party. In 1997, it captured 20 seats and regained official party status. The following year, Charest stepped down as leader, and Joe Clark returned to head the Progressive Conservative Party.

In 1987, Preston Manning had founded the Reform Party to better represent conservative values. The party failed to elect anyone in the 1988 election, but won the second largest number of seats in 1997 and formed the **Official Opposition**.

To form the government, the Reform Party needed to unite conservatives across the country. In 2000, it restructured itself under the banner of the Canadian Alliance. Manning subsequently lost the party's leadership to Stockwell Day. The Alliance only captured 62 seats in 2000, all of which were in Western Canada. As a result of this relatively poor showing, Stephen Harper, a former Reform MP, was elected leader.

In the 2000 election, the Progressive Conservative Party won only 12 seats. Three years later, the party elected Peter MacKay to replace Clark. Harper approached MacKay and persuaded him to join forces. In 2003, the Progressive Conservative Party and the Canadian Alliance agreed to form a new party—the Conservative Party of Canada. Harper became the new party's first leader just in time for the 2004 election.

In 2004, the new Conservative Party became the Official Opposition in a minority government. Eighteen months later, a non-confidence motion led to a second election. On January 23, 2006, Harper became the prime minister of a minority government, a position he retained following another election two years later. In the 2011 election, however, Harper and his Conservative Party managed to break through the barrier, winning their first majority government.

In 2003, the Progressive Conservative Party and the Canadian Alliance agreed to form a new party.

SPONSORSHIP SCANDAL

After narrowly winning the 1995 Quebec **referendum**, Liberal Prime Minister Jean Chrétien created a program to convince Quebecers that staying in Canada was worthwhile. When news leaked that the program money had been misspent, Chrétien asked Auditor General Sheila Fraser to investigate. By the time Fraser released her report, Paul Martin had succeeded Chrétien as prime minister. Fraser reported that the Liberal government had paid more than $100 million to Quebec companies for doing little work. Martin appointed Justice Charles Gomery to investigate the "sponsorship scandal." When Gomery's report was released in November 2005, the opposition parties passed a motion of non-confidence in Martin's government, and Canada went to the polls. The issue was clear, should Martin be held responsible for the scandal?

RESPONSIBLE

The opposition parties claimed that, as minister of finance, Martin should have known where the money was going. Harper said, "We have all just witnessed a sad spectacle—a prime minister so burdened with corruption in his own party that he is unable to do his job…. Do Canadians really believe that the No. 2 man in a government now under a cloud of corruption, is the person to clean up that mess today?"

NOT RESPONSIBLE

The Gomery Commission cleared Martin of all wrong doing. Its report said that most of the Cabinet, including finance minister Paul Martin, was kept in the dark about the sponsorship program. Martin explained that the finance minister's job was to provide money to the various government departments, not decide how they were to spend it.

THE RESULT

The election resulted in a Conservative minority government. Shortly thereafter, Martin resigned as Liberal leader. Harper's government passed the Accountability Act in December 2006 with new lobbying rules and reforms to prevent unethical actions and to make government transparent.

By the end of 2010, the Conservative Party under Stephen Harper had achievements in several areas.

1. The Conservatives restricted political lobbying and limited the amount of money corporations and unions could contribute to political parties.
2. The party continued to show support for the war in Afghanistan.
3. The Conservative government apologized for such past wrongs as the **Chinese Head Tax** and the **Indian Residential School System**.

Prime Minister Harper presented Phil Fontaine, the Chief of the Assembly of Nations, with a citation following the government's official apology for the abuse and cultural loss Canada's Aboriginal Peoples experienced in Indian residential schools.

TIMELINE

C anada's Conservatives have had a long, but varied, history. Even through its struggles, however, it has been able to contribute much to the country's development. The timeline below summarizes some of the key moments in Conservative Party history in Canada.

1856	1867	1873	1873
The Liberal-Conservative Party is created.	Confederation creates a country called Canada.	Following the Pacific Scandal, the Conservatives are ousted from office and Liberal Alexander Mackenzie becomes prime minister.	The Liberal-Conservative Party becomes the Conservative Party.

1878	1885	1885	1891
John A. Macdonald adopts protective tariffs.	Louis Riel leads the Métis in the North-West Resistance, an uprising against the Dominion of Canada.	John A. Macdonald allows Riel to be hanged for treason.	John A. Macdonald dies.

1911	1914–18	1917	1925
Robert Borden becomes prime minister.	World War I is fought.	An election held on the issue of conscription divides the country.	The King-Byng crisis occurs when Governor-General Byng asks Arthur Meighen to form a government.

1930			1939–45
The Conservatives come to power just as the Great Depression begins.			World War II is fought.

1942

The Conservative Party becomes the Progessive Conservative Party.

1957

Conservative John Diefenbaker ends the long Liberal control of Parliament.

1963

Diefenbaker refuses U.S. nuclear warheads.

1967

Robert Stanfield becomes leader of the Progressive Conservatives.

1976

Stanfield resigns as party leader and is replaced by Joe Clark.

1984

Brian Mulroney becomes prime minister.

1987

The Reform Party is created.

1988

Canada and the United States sign a free trade agreement.

1993

The Conservative Party experiences the biggest election loss in Canadian history.

2000

The Canadian Alliance is created from the Reform Party.

2003

The Canadian Alliance and the Progressive Conservative Party merge to become the Conservative Party of Canada.

2004

Stephen Harper becomes prime minister.

10 FAST FACTS
ABOUT THE CONSERVATIVE PARTY

1 R.B. Bennett is the only deceased prime minister not buried in Canada.

2 Sir Robert Borden was the last prime minister to accept a British knighthood.

3 John A. Macdonald started Canada's national park system in 1885, with the creation of Alberta's Banff National Park.

4 Some historians believe that the United Empire Loyalists were responsible for conservatism in early Canada. The Loyalists were people who had immigrated to the Canadas during the U.S. Revolutionary War. They had sided with Great Britain during the war and moved to the Canadas to escape persecution in the United States. Most Loyalists immigrated to what is now Ontario, where they retained their loyalty to the British Crown.

5 Today's Conservative Party supports the concept of Senate reform. Party members believe that the senators should have to be elected to the Senate. Currently, senators are chosen by the government.

6 Brian Mulroney continued his efforts at constitutional reform following the failure of the Meech Lake Accord. Another round of meetings in Charlottetown in 1991 and 1992 led to the Charlottetown Accord, which made extensive changes to the Constitution, including recognition of Quebec as a distinct society. Although it was endorsed by the three major national parties, Canadians rejected the Accord by a vote of 54 to 46 percent.

7 In 1956, the Conservative leadership convention was the first such meeting to be covered by television.

8 The Conservative Party has selected three provincial premiers as national leaders. John Bracken was the 11th premier of Manitoba, George Drew had been the 14th premier of Ontario, and Robert Stanfield had led Nova Scotia as its 17th premier.

9 Under Joe Clark, the Conservatives drafted the Freedom of Information Act, which gives Canadians the right to demand information from the federal government. The Conservatives were not in office long enough to have the act passed. It was passed by Trudeau's Liberal government as the Access to Information Act.

10 Stephen Harper is the first prime minister since Lester B. Pearson not to have attended law school.

ACTIVITY

WHAT IS A DEBATE?

When people debate a topic, two sides take a different viewpoint about one idea. They present logical arguments to support their views. Usually, each person or team is given a set amount of time to present its case. The presenters take turns stating their arguments until the total time set aside for the debate is used up. Sometimes, there is an audience in the room listening to the presentations. Later, the members of the audience vote for the person or team they think made the most persuasive arguments.

Debating is an important skill. It helps people to think about ideas thoughtfully and carefully. It also helps them develop rhythms of speech that others can follow easily.

Some schools have organized debating clubs as part of their after-school activities. Schools often hold debates in their history class or as part of studying about world events.

DEBATE THIS!

Every day, the news is filled with the issues facing Canada and its citizens. These issues are debated in the House of Commons and on city streets. People often have different views of these issues and support different solutions.

Following is an issue that has sparked discussion across the country. Gather your friends or classmates, and divide into two teams to debate the issue. Each team should take time to properly research the issue and develop solid arguments for their side.

In 1991, Prime Minister Brian Mulroney introduced Canadians to the Goods and Services Tax. The tax is placed on almost anything that Canadians purchase. While there was an initial uproar over the tax, it has now become part of Canadian life. There was much relief, however, when the tax was reduced in 2006 and then again in 2008.

Recently, there has been a movement to increase the tax once again, with the proceeds of the increase going to arts and culture programs across the country.

Should the tax be increased and spent on this type of programming?

1: When was the Conservative Party first created?

2: Who was the first Conservative prime minister?

3: What did Macdonald's Conservatives do to encourage western settlement?

4: What controversy led to MacKenzie Bowell's exit from office?

5: What is reciprocity?

6: How did Arthur Meighen become prime minister in 1926?

7: Which prime minister was responsible for developing Canada's Bill of Rights?

8: What was the Meech Lake Accord?

9: Who founded the Reform Party?

10: Which two parties merged to create today's Conservative Party?

FURTHER RESEARCH

Suggested Reading

Blake, R. *The Conservative Party*. Toronto: Random House, 1985.

Johnson, William. *Stephen Harper and the Future of Canada*. Toronto: McClelland & Stewart, 2006.

Segal, Hugh. *The Long Road Back: The Conservative Journey, 1993–2007*. Toronto: HarperCollins, 2007.

Internet Resources

Read about the Conservative Party directly from the source at **www.conservative.ca**

A detailed history of the Conservative Party can be found at **www.thecanadianencyclopedia.com**. Just type Conservative Party into the search engine.

Learn more about Canada's political parties and the election process at **www.elections.ca**

GLOSSARY

Bill of Rights: a formal summary of those rights and liberties considered essential to a people or group of people

Black Tuesday: the date of the most famous stock market crash in history

Chinese Head Tax: a fixed fee charged to each Chinese person entering Canada in the late 1800s

coalition government: a governing body formed by multiple parties who must compromise on principles

colonies: regions ruled by a country that is usually far away

Confederation: the event in 1867 when Canada became its own country

conscription: forced military service

constituencies: the districts represented by elected legislators or officials

Constitution: the set of principles and laws by which Canada is governed

constitutional monarchy: a system of government in which the powers of the ruler are restricted to those granted under the constitution and laws of the nation

Criminal Code: a group of government laws about justice, crime, and punishment

decentralization: the distribution of administrative functions or powers of a central authority among several local authorities

dominion: certain self-governing countries in the Commonwealth, such as Canada

economic depression: a period of high unemployment and low sales of products

First Nations: Canadian Aboriginal Peoples who are not Inuit or Métis

free trade: a system that allows companies to trade across national boundaries without interference from the respective governments

Great Depression: a period during the 1930s when there was a worldwide economic depression and mass unemployment

Indian Residential School system: a program that occurred from the mid-1800s to 1996 that removed First Nations children from their traditional homes to assimilate them into Euro-Canadian culture

League of Nations: an international association of states founded in 1920 and dissolved in 1946 that operated under the goal of preserving world peace

majority government: a governing party that has an absolute majority of seats in the legislature or parliament

Métis: one of Canada's Aboriginal groups; descended from First Nations women and European fur traders

minority government: a governing party that has half or fewer than half of the seats in the House of Commons or legislative assembly

Official Opposition: the second-largest party in a legislative house

private enterprise: a business unit established by private individuals for profit, instead of by or for a government or its agencies

racial quotas: a number established for immigrants of specific ethnic groups

ratify: to approve and give formal sanction to

reciprocity: the mutual exchange of trading privileges

referendum: a vote by the general public on a particular issue

responsible government: a form of government in which decisions cannot become law without the support of the majority of elected representatives

sovereignty: supreme and independent power in government as possessed by a state

tariffs: taxes on imported goods

treason: the betrayal of one's own country

treaty and status rights: the right of independence through self-determination in respect of governance, land, resources and culture

Versailles peace talks: discussions that took place in France to resolve issues from World War I

vote of confidence: a voting process in which people show support for a person or group in power

INDEX